How to Convert to Islam

How to Become a Muslim by Converting to Islam (an Islamic Religion Overview)

by Daria Masri

Table of Contents

Introduction 1

Chapter 1: Basic Beliefs of Islam 5

Chapter 2: Important Rituals of Islam 15

Chapter 3: How to Convert to Islam 31

Chapter 4: Important Holidays and Events for Muslims 39

Chapter 5: Key Pointers for Islam Converts 43

Conclusion 47

Introduction

Muslims are likely some of the most misunderstood people in the world. They are oftentimes despised for their Jihads or holy wars. So if you have decided to convert to Islam, then you must have read its true teachings about peace, love and respect. Yes, Islam is very much a religion of peace. But before you convert, you should become familiar with the Islamic beliefs and practices, and be prepared to fully incorporate these beliefs into your life. Are you ready to change your lifestyle because of Islam? Being a Muslim means embracing a new way of life.

If you choose to convert to Islam, please know that Muslims will welcome you warmly no matter your race, color, or which previous creed you belonged to. This book will help make your conversion process much easier, and will also help you to better understand and appreciate the Islamic religion.

© Copyright 2014 by LCPublifish LLC - All rights reserved.

This document is geared towards providing reliable information in regards to the topic and issue covered. The publication is sold with the idea that the publisher is not required to render accounting, officially permitted, or otherwise, qualified services. If advice is necessary, legal or professional, a practiced individual in the profession should be ordered.

- From a Declaration of Principles which was accepted and approved equally by a Committee of the American Bar Association and a Committee of Publishers and Associations.

In no way is it legal to reproduce, duplicate, or transmit any part of this document in either electronic means or in printed format. Recording of this publication is strictly prohibited and any storage of this document is not allowed unless with written permission from the publisher. All rights reserved.

The information provided herein is stated to be truthful and consistent, in that any liability, in terms of inattention or otherwise, by any usage or abuse of any policies, processes, or directions contained within is solely and completely the responsibility of the recipient reader. Under no circumstances will any legal responsibility or blame be held against the publisher for any reparation, damages, or monetary loss due to the information herein, either directly or indirectly.

Respective authors own all copyrights not held by the publisher.

The information herein is offered for informational purposes solely, and is universal as so. The presentation of the information is without contract or any type of guarantee assurance.

The trademarks that are used are without any consent, and the publication of the trademark is without permission or backing by the trademark owner. All trademarks and brands within this book are for clarifying purposes only and are the owned by the owners themselves, not affiliated with this document.

Chapter 1: Basic Beliefs of Islam

There is only one true God – Allah

It is interesting to note that Islam, Judaism and Catholicism have somewhat similar origins. In fact, Islam recognizes Adam, Moses, and Jesus Christ as prophets. A major difference is that Jews and Muslims do not acknowledge that Jesus is the Son of God, and that he was crucified and resurrected from the dead. While Islam accepts that Jesus is a true prophet, Judaism does not.

Islam means submission to the will of God. Muslims believe in one true, powerful God, Allah, who has created the universe. All types of worship and prayers are offered directly to Allah. To live a peaceful life, you should submit to the will of God. Muslims do not believe in original sin. Once you convert to Islam, Allah will forgive all your past sins, allowing you to start with a blank slate.

Muhammad is the final Prophet or Messenger of God

The Quran acknowledges Adam, Abraham, Moses and Jesus, but it declares that the final, true Prophet of God is Muhammad (also spelled Mohammed), who was sent as the messenger of Allah's teachings. Muslims are commanded to follow the teachings of Muhammad and to emulate his deeds.

The only true religion in the sight of God is Islam

Muslims firmly believe that Islam is the only true religion in the sight of God. If you are not a Muslim, you are doomed to go to hell. When you convert, you will be saved from eternal damnation. Muslims are encouraged to show respect to non-Muslims or non-believers, but they are discouraged from allowing themselves to be influenced by their non-Islam practices.

There is a heaven and a hell

To reach heaven and live a spiritual and physical life of perfection in paradise, you must follow the teachings of Islam. Muslims do good deeds and pray to earn their salvation.

The Quran is God's word

It's good to become familiar with the Quran (also called Qur'an or Koran). This book is of the same importance in the Islamic faith as the Bible is to Christians.

Just as Christians believe that the Bible is the Word of God, Muslims believe that the Quran is the Word of God. The Quran embodies the Words of God as revealed to Muhammad. The Quran is in Arabic, but you can find English versions. Included in the Quran are the same basic teachings on behavior and conduct as those taught by the majority of religions, such as thou shall not kill (except in defense of self and of Islam), thou shall not steal, obey and respect your parents, avoid fornication.

The Foundations of Muslim Life are The Five Pillars of Islam

The Five Pillars of Islam, also called the Five Pillars of Faith, serve as the framework of Muslim life. These Five Pillars include the following:

1. *Shahada or Shahadah* is the testimony of faith or daily confession of faith. Muslims

serve and obey God through the teachings of Muhammad in the Quran.

2. ***Salah or Salat*** are obligatory prayers performed 5 times a day: dawn, noon, afternoon, sunset, and nightfall. These prayers connect Muslims to God directly. Salah can be performed anywhere, but it is ideal to pray with others in a mosque. There are no priests in Islam. The prayers in the mosque can be led by any learned person called Imam, who has enough knowledge of the Quran. The congregation can decide who it will be. These prayers are spoken in the Arabic language but personal prayers can be said using your own language. If you are menstruating, or have just given birth, you are excused from the Salah. If you are not sure of the time to pray in your area, you can find the specific time for your exact location from this Islamic Finder: www.islamicfinder.org/world.php. However, take note that you must perform Wudu, a cleansing ritual or ablution, before you can say your prayers. Prayers will occupy a lot of your time as a Muslim, so be prepared for that. The steps in performing the Wudu and Salat are found in Chapter 2.

Zakat (purification and growth) - Zakat is giving support for the needy; an obligation which is clearly stated in the Quran. By giving Zakat, you purify yourself and allow spiritual growth. Since all things belong to God, Muslims believe that they are only caretakers of the blessings that they acquire. Once you convert to Islam, it is your obligation as a Muslim to purify yourself by giving 2.5% of the value of your possessions. Zakat is usually paid during the month of Ramadan. You can calculate and pay your Zakat on the following website: www.islamicity.com/mosque/zakat/Zakat_calculator.shtml.

Those who are unable to give monetary "alms tax" because of financial constraints can do so through other means, such as helping others (orphans, imams, travelers) through charity work. According to Muhammad, *"Charity is a necessity for every Muslim."*

3. ***Sawm (Fasting)*** is an obligatory fasting, from dawn to dusk, done in the month of Ramadan (9th month in the Islamic calendar) for the purpose of self-purification. For your Sawm to be valid, you should first perform the Niyyah to express your intention. Drinking and having sex is prohibited as well. Sawm ut Taam (food fasting), Sawm ul Maal (money fasting) and Sawm ul Kalam (word

fasting) are also observed. All of your activities should be focused on bringing you closer to God. You are exempted if you are sick, elderly, traveling, or nursing a baby. However, you should fast using the same number of days within the span of the year.

As a Muslim, you can also perform voluntary fasting during the following days:

- Months preceding Ramadan

- Every Monday and Thursday

- 10th day of Muharram during the Days of Asyurah (Ashura) using the Hijri calendar. You can fast before and after the 10th, too.

- 13th, 14th, and 15th day of each lunar month

- The months before Ramadan (Rajab and Shaban). You can fast as often as you want as long as you follow the rules.

- The month after Ramadan (Shawwal) (6 days)

- 9th day of Dhu al-Hijjah during the Day of Arafa using the Hijri calendar

- Non-Hajjis can fast during the first 9 days of Dhu al-Hijjah using the Islamic calendar

There are also times that you are not allowed to fast: every consecutive day of the year; during days of celebration, such as Eidul al-Adha (Festival of Sacrifice) and Eidul el-Fitr (Festival of the Fast Breaking); fasting only every Friday. If you choose to fast on Fridays, you should also fast on other days.

4. *Hajj (Pilgrimage)* is the pilgrimage to Makkah in Mecca. Muslims who are physically fit and financially able have the obligation to visit Mecca in the span of their lifetime. It will be your duty too, as a Muslim convert. Based on the Islamic calendar, the Hajj occurs from the 8th to the 12th day of Dhu al-Hijjah (last month.) You can opt for online discount offers by some Islam websites for travel packages to Mecca.

You can join Muslim pilgrims from all over the world to perform a series of rituals. The first ritual is to walk seven times in a counterclockwise direction around the Ka'aba. (The Ka'aba is where Muslims face every time they pray. It is where Muhammad conducted his last teachings.) Your next activity is to run back and forth between the hills of Safa and Marwa seven times.

The last ritual requires you to stand on the desert of Arafat with your Muslim brothers to join in prayer for God's forgiveness. The following day, pilgrims throw 7 pea-sized pebbles at 3 white pillars as a symbol of Stoning the Devil. This activity, however, has caused a number of stampedes throughout the years, killing hundreds of pilgrims, so the activity has been modified.

Every Muslim has to take the pilgrimage at least once in their lifetime, so do not miss this chance to be with your Muslim brothers from all corners of the earth. Mecca is a hot and humid place but nowadays Mecca provides pilgrims with clean water, air-conditioning inside the buildings, and amenities that will allow you to relax and concentrate on being at peace with God.

The festival 'Id al-Adha marks the end of the Hajj, with Muslim communities all over the world celebrating through gift-giving and prayers.

Chapter 2: Important Rituals of Islam

Islam has essential rituals that Muslims reverently observe. If you are experiencing difficulty in reading and speaking the Arabic prayers, a brother Muslim from your congregation can help you. You can also enlist the assistance of online websites for Muslim converts. Most Muslim rituals include prayers, so be sure to set time aside for this.

The following prayer rituals are generally used when performing the Salat, one of the Five Pillars of Islam.

The Wudu

The Wudu is a mental preparation done before the Salat. You can follow these steps:

Step #1 - Perform the Niyyah (intention)

Perform the Niyyah (Niyah) focusing on the fact that you are doing it for God. You can mentally or orally say "Bismillah", meaning "In the Name of Allah". While doing this, try to attain a peaceful state. This is the stage where your focus should only be on your prayer. You should be one with God.

Step #2 – Wash your hands

Using water, first wash your right hand with your left hand. Ascertain that you wash your hand up to the wrist and between your fingers, rubbing thoroughly to dislodge all dirt. Then wash your left hand with your right, in the same manner.

Step #3 – Rinse your mouth

With your right hand, cup water into your mouth and rinse your mouth thoroughly. Do this 3 times.

Step #4 – Sniff water into your nose

With your right hand, splash or sniff water into your nostrils and then blow. You can use your left hand to blow your nose 3 times.

Step #5 – Wash your face

Wash your whole face by cupping your hands from your right ear to your left and from your forehead to your chin. Do this 3 times.

Step #6 – Wash your arms and elbows

Remember, the sequence is always right before left, so wash your right arm from wrist up to your elbow. Then wash your left arm and elbow the same way. Do this 3 times for each arm. Each inch of skin from your arms to your elbows should be washed. While washing, the hands should be held upwards to avoid getting them dirty again.

Step #7 – Pass your wet palms over your head

Pass your wet palms over your head starting from your eyebrows going backwards to the nape of your neck. Do this only once.

Step #8 – Include your ears and the area behind your ears

Pass the wet index fingers of both hands into the opening of each ear, with each thumb passing over the area underneath your ears. Do both ears simultaneously.

Step #9 – Wash your feet

Wash your feet by starting with your right foot. Take care to wash up to the ankles and in between your toes. Do this 3 times. Follow the same procedure with your left foot.

Step #10 – Recite the prayer of witness

You can now recite this prayer:

"Ash-hadu la ilaha illallahu wa ash-hadu anna Muammadan 'abduhu wa rasuluhu." (I testify that there is no God but Allah and He is One and has no partner, and I also testify that Muhammad is His chosen servant and true messenger.)

Wudu can be nullified by the following:

- Bloody discharge from any part of the body

- Discharges such as urine, feces, dog saliva, sputum

- Falling asleep

- Falling unconscious

- Vomiting foul substances

- Sexual intercourse - A different purification called Ghusul (ghusl) is performed by including your private parts when washing.

You must be thinking of how inconvenient it is to do the Wudu every time you do the Salah, especially if you are wearing socks and shoes, or if you are travelling. If you are wearing socks, you can renew your Wudu by wiping the cover of each foot once, instead of washing your feet. This is applicable within a period of 24 hours. If you are travelling, you can observe this method for 3 days. Performing the Wudu will become easier with practice.

The Salat

After you have completed your Wudu, you' are ready to say your Salat. There are a few dress requirements for praying the Salat. For males, the clothing should cover the shoulders and the lower portion of the body. For females, clothing that covers the whole body, including the head, is preferable. The face, hands, and front of the feet need not be covered. The clothing should be free from feces, urine, blood, or dog's saliva. The place of prayer should also be clean.

Step #1 – Stand and face the Qiblah or Ka'bah or Makkah in Mecca

In North America, the direction of the Qiblah is usually facing the east with a little angle to the north. If you are located somewhere else, other than North America, and you are not sure which way to face, you can use the Qiblah Locator (www.qiblalocator.com). Your feet should also be spaced evenly with your hands at your sides and your head bowed down.

Step #2 – Express your prayer's Niyyah or intention

This is where you express your intention for your prayers to God. Prayers are your direct lines to God, where your whole being is in communion with Him, so do it fully focused mentally, physically, and spiritually. You can recite your prayers in a voice that is not too loud or too soft, or you can say it soundlessly. If an Imam is leading when you are inside a mosque, you can say your Niyyah silently.

You must also state what type of prayer you will be reciting and the number of Rakaats (Rakats or Raka'ats). A Rakaat is a single unit of Islamic prayer, and each type of prayer has a number of obligatory Rakaat. The dawn prayer, called Fajr, consists of 2 Rakaats. The midday and late afternoon prayers, Zuhr and Asr, require 4 Rakaats, while the evening prayer, Maghrib, requires 3 Rakaats. The last prayer of the day, the Isha, has 4 Rakaats and 3 Rakaats of the witr.

There are also Friday prayers composed of 2 Rakaats. This prayer is usually done in a mosque.

Step #3 – Do the Takbiratul Ihram

The Takbiratul Ihram is done by raising your arms in line with your ear lobes for men, and in line with the shoulders, for women. Your palms should be facing forward. Recite the prayer "Allahu Akbar" (God is The Greatest).

Step #4 – Do the Qiyam

For men, the arm is lowered below the navel with the right hand over the left. For women, the right hand is over the chest. There are various positions for women depending on their Islam sects. Shia and Malikis women leave their hands hanging at their sides. Hanbali, Hanafi and Shafi'I have their hands folded. You should bow your head with your eyes on the ground.

Recite the Al-Fatihah prayer of opening Surah of the Quran. You can memorize Surahs from the Quran. These are brief prayers, which you can easily commit to memory.

Step #5 – Do the Ruk'u

The Ruk'u is done by dropping your hands and placing them over your knees. You then bow looking at your feet. Make sure that your body/back is parallel to the ground. Your head should be in line with your back. As you bend say "Allahu Akbar". Afterwards, recite this line 3 times: "Subhanna rabbiyal 'Azeem" (Holy is my Lord, the Magnificent), while remaining bent. You can also say this prayer 3 times: "Subhan rabbi alAdheem" (All praise to Allah, the Great).

Step #6 – Rise to standing position

Rise to a standing position while saying, "Sami' allaahu liman hamidah" (Allah listens to him who praises him), followed with "Rabbanaa wa lakal hamd" (Our Lord, to You is due all praise). When you are back to your standing position say, "Allahu Akbar" (God is The Greatest).

Step #7 – Prostrate yourself

With your hands on your knees, kneel down slowly and press your palms, nose, and forehead on the ground. Your nose should be pressed firmly without hurting yourself. Be careful not to lower your elbows. Both of your toes should be bent facing Qibla. If you are a woman your elbows may be lowered to touch the ground. Then recite this 3 times: "Subhaana rabbiyal 'Alaa" (Glory be to my Lord, the Most high), followed with "Allahu Akbar".

Step #8 – Sit up

If you are a woman you should sit up with your soles up and under your body. If you are a man, you should sit with your heel turned up and your right toes bent. Pause for a while before saying "Allahu Akbar" (God is The Greatest).

Step #9 – Prostrate yourself again

Repeat step #7 while saying "Allahu Akbar" (God is The Greatest).

Step #10 – Rise to a Jalsa (sitting) or Qayam (standing) position

As you are rising to your position, say "Allahu Akbar". Pause for a while. You are now ready for your second Rakaat. Repeat steps #1 to #9, excluding step #3 (Takbiratul Ihram).

After the second prostration, sit on your left leg, with your right foot upward. Place your right hand on your right thigh with your fingers balled in a fist, except for your index finger, which should be pointing forward. Your left hand should be resting on your left thigh. Recite the Tashahhud (Tahiyat) mentally, followed by the Salawat (Salawaat), and then the Durud (Durood). The Tashahhud should be done after the second or last Rakaat. There are some variants of the Tashahhud depending on the type of Muslim; whether Sunni, Shi'a (Shia), Sufi, or Ahmadiyya.

If you want to do another Rakaat, repeat the same steps as the second Rakaat but don't say the Salaam and the Durud.

Step #11 – Say the Salaam or Tasleem

The Salaam is said facing the right, and then said again facing the left. This prayer is addressed to the angel recording your rightful deeds (right), and the angel recording your wrongful deeds (left). The characters in Arabic are to give you an example of what they look like. You say:

السلام عليكم ورحمة الله وبركاته (Peace and blessings of God be upon you.)

Step #12 – Say your personal prayers

After the obligatory Rakaat, you can now say your personal prayers in your own language, while cupping your hands over your chest and then wiping your face with your hands.

Whew! Seems difficult to do, right? But you will get the hang of it. Do not be in a rush. Praying the Muslim way takes time to learn.

The Tashahhud

This is done after the second and the last Rakaat during the Salat.

> At-tahiy-yatu lillahi was sala-watu wat-tay yibatu As-salamu 'alayka ay-yuhan-nabiy-yuwa rahma tullahi wa bara-katuhu. Asalamu 'alayna wa'ala 'I badila his As-salamu 'alayna wa'ala 'inadila his-sali-heen Ash hadu al-la ilaha il-lal lahu wa ash hadu an-na Muhammadan 'a-duhu wa rasuluh.

> (Greetings! All worships; physical, oral, and monetary are for Allah. Peace be upon you, Oh Prophet and Allah's mercy and blessings. Peace be on us and on all righteous servants of Allah. I bear witness that no one is worthy of worship except Allah, and I bear witness that Muhammad is His servant and Messenger.)

The Salawat

> This type of Muslim prayer is usually spoken after the Tashahhud. There are various kinds of Salawat. The most common is "Allahumma

salli ala Muhamadin wa ala ali Muhammad" and "Sallallahu alayhi wassallam".

(May Allah send His praise, mercy and forgiveness upon Muhammad and his family.)

The Durud (Durood)

The Durud is a prayer for everyone. One example is the Durood Nariyah, which goes:

As Salaam Alaykum wa Rahmatullahi wa Barakatuh. (May Allah's peace, mercy and blessings be upon you all.)

Chapter 3: How to Convert to Islam

Converting to Islam is easy. All you have to do is say the Shahada sincerely, and you are already a Muslim. Now as a Muslim, there are 2 general categories that you should try to really focus on incorporating into your life: prayers and good deeds. They are equally important.

If you truly believe that Islam is the religion for you, then here are specific steps you can follow to convert to Islam.

Step #1 - Read more about Islam

This is your first step because you should have the correct reasons for converting to Islam. Knowing what Islam is all about, and what the religion stands for, is crucial. Learning more about the beliefs and practices from the Quran will familiarize you with what to expect.

Step #2 – Prepare yourself mentally

Free yourself of any vestiges of your previous religious beliefs. Empty your mind and be at peace with yourself. Start with a completely blank slate. Be ready to open your mind towards the teachings and beliefs of Islam. Muslims always state their intentions before any activity, so be clear about your intentions too.

Step #3 – Take a shower to cleanse yourself

Taking a shower before your Shahada is a symbolic way of cleansing your body and soul of impurities. You can also take a shower after your Shahada, but some prefer to do this before the Shahada because they feel purer in spirit while reciting the prayer. You should also clip your nails and shave the hair under your armpits and pubic hair. Wear clean clothes and say your prayer in a clean place free from urine, feces, blood, and dog's saliva.

Step #4 - Say your Shahada (Shahadah) or Testimony of Faith

You can do this alone, in a mosque, or with a brother Muslim. The Shahada indicates that you are accepting Allah as your one, true God, with Muhammad as His Messenger. Say this testimony sincerely and wholeheartedly:

"La ilaha illa Allah, Muhammad raoolu Allah."

(There is no true God but Allah, and Muhammad is the Messenger of Allah.)

As soon as you have pronounced this Testimony of Faith, all your past sins are erased and forgiven. You are now like a newborn infant, pure and clean. Strive to maintain this purity by performing your prayers and rituals religiously and doing good deeds.

Step #5 – Start reading the Quran

Although you may have read some portions of the Quran already, start reading again. In fact, the Quran must be your daily "news". It will educate you about all the religious practices and beliefs of Islam. It represents the word of God through His Prophet, Muhammad, so you have to know it like the back of your hand.

In the Quran, you will read about how to deal with non-Muslims, how to manage your financial affairs, how to treat your Muslim brothers, and many more vital information that will make you closer to God. If you cannot understand Arabic, you can surf online for legitimate Muslim websites that can help you.

Step #6 – Perform your daily Muslim prayers

Muslims consider prayers as a pivotal part of their lives. Their daily activities always include the Salat (daily obligatory prayers). You are a Muslim now, so start performing your Islam rituals. From now on, Salats should also be the center of your daily life. You will achieve peace and calmness.

Step #7 – Obtain a "Certificate of Islam"

Ordinarily you do not need this certificate, but if you are to fulfill one of your obligations, the Hajj (Pilgrimage), then you will need it. You can show your certificate to prove that you are a Muslim. This is because only Muslims are allowed to enter Mecca. It would be best to have one with you when you travel.

Step #8 – Find a Mosque or community

It will help you tremendously if you have a Muslim community that you can belong to. Your Muslim brothers can help you with your religious rituals. If there are no Muslim communities in your area, you can surf online for good Muslim websites that can help you prosper as an Islam convert.

Step #9 – Live as a Muslim

You can find essential pointers in the Quran on how to live as a Muslim. You must completely submit your life to Allah. Some of these are:

- Perform your daily Salat

- Do not eat pork meat and Haram (forbidden) foods

- Adapt the Muslim way of dressing modestly. For women, clothes covering the head and body are appropriate. Wearing a Hijab (to cover your entire body) and Nijab (face cover) is advisable. The clothes should be loose so that your figure will not be outlined. Your clothes should not attract unnecessary attention to your body shape. Sometimes, the Nijab may not be worn, depending on the area you are in.

For men, the navel to the knee should be covered. Clothing for Muslim men is not as strict as that of women. The Quran emphasized that women should be protected.

- Do not shake the hand of a woman who is not a relative. Hugging a non-relative is prohibited as well. Considered as relatives are parents, grandparents, children, uncles and aunts, nephews and nieces. Cousins are not counted as relatives.

- Eat with your right hand, and wash your private parts with your left.

- Do not flirt or have sex with anyone except your husband or wife.

- Avoid wearing clothes soiled with urine, feces, blood, or dog's saliva.

These are only a few of the practices that you should follow. It is easy to convert to Islam. The challenge, though, is in maintaining your being a Muslim. The daily obligatory prayers can be taxing for you, particularly if your previous lifestyle and religion have never included prayers that must be performed five times daily. However, there are significant advantages to being a Muslim. You will live a healthier lifestyle because eating pork and drinking are prohibited. Your life will be about prayers and doing good deeds, which will result in positive vibes and good karma.

Chapter 4: Important Holidays and Events for Muslims

Muslim holidays can be counted on your fingers. There are two major Muslim holidays; the Eidul al-Adha ('Id al-Adha) and the Eidul el-Ftr (Eid Ul-Ftr).

Eidul al-Adha (Festival of Sacrifice) is the celebration after the Hajj.

Eidul el-Fitr (Festival of the Fast Breaking) is the celebration of the end of Ramadan. Muslims express their gratitude to God for his blessings during the fasting period. These are celebrated by Muslims worldwide.

Ramadan is the month of fasting and abstinence to become closer to God done on the 9th month in the Islamic calendar. You fast from dawn to dusk. This involves not only fasting from eating, drinking and sex, but also from unwanted traits that you, as a Muslim, should eschew. This is meant to strengthen your relationship with God.

Day of Ashura – This day commemorates the martyrdom of Muhammad's grandson, Hussein, and is observed on the 10th day of Muharram. This is observed primarily by Shi'ite Muslims.

Al Hijira (Islamic New Year) – This is considered the Islamic New Year because it celebrates Muhammad's migration from Mecca to Medina.

Lailat al Qadr (Night or Power) commemorates the night that Allah revealed the Quran to Muhammad.

Milad un Nabi (Shia) – Celebration of the birthday of Muhammad. The dates vary because Sunnis celebrate it 5 days earlier, while the Shia Muslims celebrate it 5 days later. The other types of Muslims do not believe in celebrating it.

Hajj (Pilgrimage) – This event is described in detail in Chapter 1.

Chapter 5: Key Pointers for Islam Converts

The Islam religion welcomes anyone to become a convert no matter what religion he or she previously belonged to. Muslims believe that Islam is the only true religion and that non-Muslims will suffer "Hellfire" if they do not convert.

For your complete successful conversion, here are significant pointers that you ought to adopt:

1. **Join Muslim support groups**

    It can be lonely sometimes when your non-Muslim family and friends are not with you in your endeavor. You need a support group that will understand and help you with your religious obligations. You can join online groups if there are no local support groups in your area. Stay away from extremists, whether from the extreme conservative or the extreme liberals. Extreme beliefs may result in violence and crime.

2. **Treat non-Muslims with respect**

Most likely you will be treated indifferently by your non-Muslim family and friends when you convert to Islam. This is due to the bad image that some Muslim extremists have projected to the world. Nevertheless, you will have to treat them with respect and do as the Quran dictates; respect your parents and show love and concern to your family and friends. You will need to understand that all they want is your safety, well-being, and happiness.

3. **All that you do is a form of worship to God**

Every action, every word, every prayer is a form of worship, henceforth, you should be conscious of everything you do.

4. **Belief and good deeds are the basic requirements for Islam**

When you fulfill these two, you are well on your way to becoming a good Muslim. Your religion is the true religion, and when you perform your obligations your entry into heaven will be assured. You should not have any doubt that this is the truth. If you doubt this, then Islam is not for you.

5. **Duas (supplications) for the Wudhu, should not be done in bathrooms with toilets**

You should do the Duas outside of the bathroom if it has a toilet. However, you can read your Duas inside the bathroom (without a toilet). To prevent wetting your prayer copy, you can wrap it in plastic or you can laminate it. This will make it more convenient for you to bring it into your bathroom.

Conclusion

Converting to Islam is to your advantage if you believe in your heart and soul that it is the right religion for you. The practices and beliefs of Islam prove that it is a religion of peace, love, and respect. The actions of a few extremists have associated Muslims with terrorists. The truth, however, is that the majority of Muslims are peace-loving people who observe the universal laws practiced by almost all religions on earth.

On American and European soil, you may experience becoming isolated or despised because of your decision. Do not react with enmity and rancor, but follow the rules of the Quran – treat them with respect and love. This will show non-believers that you have not been mistaken in converting to Islam.

As-salamu alaykum. (Peace be upon you.)

Last, I'd like to thank you for purchasing this book! If you enjoyed it or found it helpful, I'd greatly appreciate it if you'd take a moment to leave a review on Amazon. Thank you!

Printed in Great Britain
by Amazon